COWS
VS
RHINOS

KHATIB ALI

CONTENTS

CONTENT

INTRODUCTION

The symbolism of cows versus rhinos were true for me throughout my entire life. It's the things that I saw, the things that I did, and the things that I was told to do. Truth be told, the things that others that were semi successful, told me to do, slowed my life down! In fact, I'm going to embellish, a little bit. Listening to most of them, pretty much put my life to a complete halt in regards to my purpose. I'm not even going to talk to you about the slow up of my success. This story really made me think about myself. I went through hell in the early stages of my life. I had to develop into a rhino. When I share this story in my sales training seminars all across the country. I am continuously reminded of those trials of my past. We can't go forward in the future without remembering the hardships we've been through.

Our past makes us stronger. I tell people all the time, if you don't discipline yourself now someone or something will discipline you. God willing this book will take you through a paradigm shift in your life as the words that I write down took me through a paradigm shift of my own. I remember being told by a friend when I was going through some legal trouble that God doesn't call the qualified, he qualifies the called. This stuck with me my entire life! This was about 15 years ago.

How many of you reading this book believe that success and purpose go hand-in-hand? When you travel down the pages of this book you will find that you have something in you that is greater than your current circumstance. You will come to believe fully that whatever the mind can conceive the mind will believe and bring forth everything you want into your physical reality just like it did for me.

KHATIB ALI

LESSON 1

IT'S EASIER TO BE RICH

Why is it easier to be rich?

Let me ask you a question, is it easier to be rich or is it easier to be poor? Most people will get this question wrong. I am creating a mind-shift for you, which most people refer to as a paradigm shift. Most people will say it's easier to be poor. That's wrong. In life you have to work extremely hard to be poor. Let me explain. Our mindset is that **"poor"** means someone homeless or living on the street, that's not poor. That's being homeless, being out there. Poor simply means Passing Over Opportunities Repeatedly. That is one of my favorite acronyms. Someone that is homeless may need help, when I say poor, I mean when you have more months left at the end of your money. I hear people all the time say, I'm just trying to make ends meet, when people don't realize that it's impossible to make ends meet, when ends are going in two different directions. I want you to understand we are in a rat race. You are going against every single person in America. Think globally, but I will use America as an example.

We are in competition starting the day we're born and inundated with expectations throughout our lifetime. A lot of times, these expectations include people asking what you want to do? What do you want to be when you grow up? Most children will say the cute thing, doctor, lawyer, a police officer, etc. That may not really be what they want. It may be what they think people want to hear. Let me tell you why it is hard to be poor. You are in competition with so many people. This is the 97% rule. You are in competition with 97% of the population - thus meaning you are competing with the majority. By contrast, the reason it is easier to be rich is that you are only in competition with 3% of the population. As an example, when you graduate from high school, you are competing with everyone that has a diploma, and everyone else with a higher level of education. Also, if you were to go online to a job site, that job site allows you to put application after application. You have some people that put in 5 applications, some put in 10, so on and so forth. You are competing against everyone that applies. And this is how you get jobs in our society.

Another acronym I will mention is JOB - Journey Of the Broke or Just Over Broke. You are sitting down and doing applications and typically, some take an hour, some take two hours, some you can quick apply and apply to 100 jobs in an instant. Now we even have social media platforms like Linked In for instance. At the end of the day you are in competition with every single applicant. Some people might be better than us, some people might have a higher education, but we are still in the rat race applying for the job. How long does it take you to secure the job for which you apply? Sometimes it may take you 3 weeks, a month, but you are getting paid for that? The answer is no - you are not getting paid for that. You are doing all that work and you are not getting paid.

I see it happen all the time. Especially since 2008. Hypothetically, on the flip side, a rich person that thinks rich - being rich is not just having money in your pockets. Being rich is being fearless, being rich is being a rhino. So, if we take all those hours in the day that it takes you to apply for a job - why can't you do something, like sell something? You can do something that you love and transform that into making income. If you have some type of product - put the money up. It doesn't have to be a lot of money. It can be $500. Take that product and sell it. Let me give you an example, a well known artist packed the trunk of his car full of CDs, he went to every single gas station in New Orleans and beyond and sold those CDs for profit and started a very popular company called No Limit Records - which created millions for himself and his entire family. Most of you reading this book are either in sales or don't want to sell, and that's okay. But I want to help you understand that every single day in life we are selling something.

We are always selling ourselves. Those of you that are married, you had to sell yourselves to your husband or your wife. And when I say you sold yourself to your spouse, I mean, there are things we did before that marriage happened, that person was sold on us. So, I want you to understand that every day in life, we are selling, even if we don't think we are.

The reason I am telling you it is easier to be rich, is simply because you have less competition. You are only competing with 3% of the population, versus competing with 97% of the population. And we do it again and again, time and time again, doing what it is they want us to do versus what we want to do for ourselves. One of the big things blocking us from success is the fact that we keep doing things over and over again and expecting a different result. We all know that is the definition of insanity. As a cow, 97% of the population has been taught to go to school, get a good education, land a great job, and retire. As a 3% person, which is a rhino, you are taught to think freely, own a business, invest, and become an owner. The cows go through what I call a **40/40/40** plan.

It simply means we work for 40 years, for 40 hours a week, and we get paid only 40% of the money we were making when we retire, but let me ask you a question. Would you all agree that we get better in time? The man that thinks the same way in his thirties as he did in his twenties has lost 10 years of his life. Yet the system of slaughter has led us to believe that the older that we get the less valuable we become. 97% of cows graze in the pastures, one cow eats grass and the next cow eats grass too. If one cow moos, then the other cow moos. I want you to think about the system as the cowboy or the guy that herds the cattle. 97% of the population is the herd.

They moo, all over the place. If someone hits the cow with a negativity arrow, it penetrates. The arrow of doubt hits the cow too - that is because cows typically have thin skin. When the cowboy comes and starts herding the cattle, we all know what that means. We all know where they are going. And they just follow, because guess what, that's what our parents told us to do. We all know what's ahead of us. The slaughter house.

The funny thing about life is that we see the slaughter house ahead of us. We have seen our parents do things they don't want to do - even though we have seen our parents work hard and most of us are proud of their accomplishments, the question would be: is that what you want to do? Is that what you want your life to be? And that is where the slaughter house comes in. And we all know what happens at the slaughter house - most dreams end up in the graveyard. The rhino eats grass, the rhino grazes in the pastures, but the difference is it develops thick skin.

When a negative arrow or an arrow of doubt hits the rhino, it bounces right off. The difference between the rhino and a cow, is that when the herder comes they are not going to use a lasso. In fact, they may have to pull out a bazooka gun, because it's a rhino. But what many people don't understand - if you move with the fearless heart of a rhino, nothing can stop you. In fact, nothing can actually touch you because most rhinos are endangered species. Hence, why the rich are 3% of the population.

If you are fearless anything that gets in your way cannot stop you. Even in the rhino's case, when hit with the bazooka gun, because it is protected. Even though you may be scared, even though you may have to take a leap of faith, understand that God will always be with you and protect you and guide you if you think like a rhino.

LESSON 2
HOW MONEY IS MADE

We've all heard the saying, money is the root of all evil. Well, I want to correct this saying because money is not the root of all evil. The truth of the matter is worshiping money is the root of all evil! I want to break this down very simply, we have to learn how to get money to work for us. Money is an object. It is a piece of paper, we have to learn how to channel money in our direction. It's kind of like oxygen. The reason we feel this way is because we have a fear of money.

If you make money you don't want to spend it, if you lose money your world is over. But the way to increase money is to understand money is our friend and is capable of multiplying, if we understand how money is made. You see, we have to understand it's not the greenback stamps that drive us, it's what the money can buy us that drives us. How the money can take care of family members can also drive us. 9 times out of 10, most marriages would be successful if we all know, 65 to 70 percent of marriages end because of finances.

I want to tell you a quick story that my mentor told me a long time ago. This is a true story. A stay at home mom a homemaker asked her husband if she could have 10 dollars. And her husband replied to her, what for? That question stunned her and from that point she made a decision never to have to ask anyone for money ever again and she became a multi-millionaire through her own business. I tell you that story because it hits home for most people. At that point, that woman understood what she brought to the marketplace. And for the husband to ask that question, she knew what she brought to the marketplace to her husband.

So what do you bring to the marketplace? What skills do you have? What dreams do you have? One of the main secrets of how money is made starts with desire. Desire is the starting point of all achievement. Think about it - What do you bring to the marketplace? There is a big difference between a person that makes $1,000 a month and a person that makes $10,000 a month. I want you to remember that you can't change your destination overnight, but you can change your direction overnight. So, the challenge of life is, you can have more than you've got if you become more than you are. So, the person that makes $1,000 a month is simply accepting to be average versus the person making $10,000 they both have the same opportunity, business, company, but they have a totally different financial position.

The difference between the two is **attitude**. I once heard a quote from Warren Buffet that said, "your attitude determines your latitude". So, it's your attitude and how you perceive yourself along with faith that drives the income that you make. In most experiences in life, we have to understand that your income will never exceed your personal development. I want to share the notion of manifestation. It's very simple, you don't get what you want in life, you get what you picture.

Understand this, if you want a Lamborghini, it's going to take money to get it. But you don't think about money to get the Lamborghini. You think about the Lamborghini. So, we put the picture of what we want, who we want to be, and where we want to be in our mind until it becomes a burning desire and manifest in your life. So, unless you grow, the money that you want is going to be too far out of reach. When I was growing up, as a kid, after football season, I would sometimes get home early from school.

Like most kids, I would sit in front of the TV, which I now call the electronic income reducer, grab some chips or any snack I can find out of the cabinet. And when I turn the TV on, there would be a cartoon on called duck-tales. What really interested me, is at the start of the cartoon, Scrooge McDuck would be swimming through a pool of money. He had a vault full of money that he would just swim through.

As a young boy I would look at that in amazement. Everyone else may have been looking at the cartoon, I was looking at Scrooge McDuck, saying I want to be that guy swimming in a pool of gold. And if you truly know of Scrooge McDuck, he gained his happiness from helping people and yet he would take time out and swim through his money. How many of you want to be like Scrooge McDuck? The reason I am mentioning this, is because there are a lot of things that we see in our life that drives our brain to want to accomplish more.

My all-time favorite TV show, don't laugh at me when I share this, is the Lifestyles Of The Rich And Famous. When I watched the TV show, it took me to a different place. And I always asked the question why? Why are they so happy? Why are they living champagne riches and caviar dreams? Why are my parents working 80 hours a week and when they come home they aren't happy. Because the 3% has got it figured out.

Happiness does not come from money, it comes from the ability to understand how money works for you. If we understand this, we will always have money and we will be happy knowing we are leaving a legacy for our children's grandchildren and their grandchildren's grandchildren. In closing, I am going to ask this question one more time. What do you bring to the marketplace? Write down your pros and write down your cons - and be honest with yourself. Pros on the left, cons on the right - draw a line down the center of the paper - what are your strengths and what are your weaknesses? And then determine for yourself how to improve on your weaknesses and how to use your strengths to add value to those weaknesses. And then write down, what you think you bring to the marketplace. Whether it's at your job, whether it is your business, whether it's with your relationships, your friendships, and watch money start flowing to you.

We have been taught by our parents, our religious leaders, the church, schools, etc. that money is the root of all evil when in fact, they have been wrong this whole time. So I appeal to you, to lose the notion that money is the root of all evil.

LESSON 3
SELL YOUR ARM

Sell me your arm! Would you let me buy your right arm for a million dollars? All I want to do, is take a sharp razor blade and cut your arm off, the doctor is right there and I will give you a million bucks for it. How many of you would sell me your arm for a million dollars? I know what you're thinking - I'm not selling you my arm for a million dollars by the way my arm is way more valuable than a million bucks! And some of you might be thinking (to yourself), yeah, I'll sell you my arm for a million dollars.

There are two types of people, the person that is going to sell me their arm and the person that's not going to sell me their arm. It's a simple question and the only way you can answer it is will you do it or will you not do it. If you ask me, I would sell you my arm immediately for a million dollars. I know you may be saying to yourself this dude is crazy as hell. But I will tell you, the majority of the 3% would sell you their arm immediately and let me explain to you why? One of the biggest cities in the country is New York City - Manhattan.

A census came out and there were about 500 or so millionaires in NYC. There would be more than that by now, but let's go with that figure. 500 millionaires in NYC. We would agree that 500 millionaires in a city that large isn't a lot of millionaires. So, the hopes of becoming a millionaire doesn't come to a lot of people. There are people working jobs, in school paying tuition people doing a lot of things except becoming millionaires. Most people don't understand what it takes to become one, but most people want to become one. So,

I ask people this very serious question, when they are working that job that makes them stay away from their families for a minimum of 40 hours a week.

I want to help you understand that you are selling your arms, you are selling your legs, you are selling your heart, in fact, you are selling your soul including your personal time freedom. This is called intellectual property. And most people in the 97% category are doing it for minimum wage. But yet, when I ask you to sell that one arm to me, you don't want to. Because you are guided by the worst sin of all, **fear**. Let me break this down for you. When I say you are guided by fear, of course you are going to be scared to get your arm cut off, but I can ask any mother or father, that's reading this book right now, would you jump in front of a bullet for your child? And the answer would be yes! But yet, in the real world of things, and in the big scheme of things, would you really jump, in front of a bullet for your child? Wouldn't you give up your arm for a million dollars if it was to sacrifice for your family! I hope you understand what I am getting at.

Because we say we love our children, our family, wife, husband, but yet we won't do whatever it takes to be successful. So, I am kidding with you about cutting off your arm, but in retrospect, I am simply telling you that in order for you to be successful and become a millionaire, even before you make a million dollars, you've got to be fearless you have to be willing to sacrifice something! This is the difference between a millionaire and someone making minimum wage. Because if you aren't willing to do whatever it takes for your Why - which is your mother, your father, your wife, your husband, your children, your future, your legacy, you will not be successful. So, I am going to ask this question one more time, would you sell me your arm for a million dollars? I am going to take it a step further. I want you to draw a picture in your mind. There are two tall buildings. There is a building on the left and one on the right. You are on the building to the left and the building on the right is burning.

You can see that it is burning and you can see money bags on the top of that burning building. Would you jump onto that building and risk your life to save those money bags from burning? Only if you were crazy would you say yes - but let me ask you this question. If we replace these money bags with your children, or your parents, would you jump over to that building to try and save them - the answer is yes. You can see the difference. This is what we call a paradigm shift. The reason I explain it to you this way - because a lot of us say that we would do everything in our power to make sure our children have what they want. To make sure our parents are taken care of when they get older.

But do we really take the necessary leaps to make sure that were are giving our all to our loved ones, that we are giving our all to ourselves? Fear is that one thing that keeps us from realizing our goals and dreams. So, in this chapter I am asking and pleading with you that you have to be fearless. As if your life and your children's lives depended on it. Let's stop being selfish. Asking you the question about cutting off your arm wasn't really about me wanting you to cut your arm off - it's for you to understand how selfish we are subconsciously. How selfish we are when we don't live the way God intended for us to live.

KHATIB ALI

LESSON 4
BE YOUR OWN BOSS

I am asked all the time about how you can be your own boss. Simply, how can one go about owning their own business? Some people don't understand the difference between being self-employed and being a business owner. But like I've said before, you don't have to be great to start, but you have to start to be great. So, let's talk about the employee. I want to begin by saying I am not at all against working for someone else. We all have to start somewhere and there is value in on the job training. I definitely feel like this helps you build yourself up in business.

The biggest problem I see in working for others is the loss of your own dreams and the continuous cycle of making others rich and putting your dreams on hold while helping them realize theirs. I learned a lot of valuable skills in the workforce that prepared me for entrepreneurship such as leadership (Marines), public speaking (multi-level marketing), Sales (Auto Industry), Discipline (Marines), Time Management (Auto Industry), Working with others (all of the above), Management (Auto Industry), Team Building (Marines/ MLM), *Personal Development (MLM). I understand that without the ability to train on these things by using my J.O.B. I would not be as successful today.

I'll also be honest and say I wasn't the best employee either. Lol, - I think we learn valuable skills while on the J.O.B. but we have to learn how to be fearless and take the skills that we learn and apply it to something we can create for ourselves and for legacies to come within our family. I understand that being your own boss isn't for everyone, so I'm simply speaking to those that endeavor on the not so easy task of being self-sufficient. Those that don't want to depend on someone else for your well-being. I loved the aspect of Auto Sales when I was in the work force because I always told myself when I walk through the doors of this dealership that I am simply a percentage partner of the owner of the dealership. I earned anywhere from 25% up to 35% of the gross profit of each vehicle I sold and that was simply one way we got paid in that industry.

The upside was that I didn't have to pay for an office, a computer, a phone or the cars that were available for sale. The downside were the hours away from home and the fact that someone could still work against me (The Manager), which happened often as I made more money than most of them. One thing I absolutely hate about corporate America is the fact that you don't get to choose who you work with and eventually every morning or evening when you leave becomes a prayer service (of you wanting to quit or not wanting to beat up or curse out a coworker or your manager).

The best thing I ever did in my life in 2007 was resign from my J.O.B. and it was also the scariest thing I ever did. This was a point in my life where I learned you can make a lot of money in a recession. I resigned from my J.O.B. because I kept working with customers that were not only making money in a recession but I felt like they were on recess. They were buying 300k plus cars cash in 2007 go figure. I knew that I had to hook my wagon to these business people. I remember a gentleman by the name of Larrye Cheaves (he later became a close friend and business partner). He asked me a question I will never forget. He said: Khatib I know you're doing well for yourself right now but God forbid, if you were to walk outside right now and got hit by a car.

How are you gonna maintain your current lifestyle? He said if you're making 200k + here what do you think you can do with 100% of your income from your own efforts? Better yet after you truly learn the art of business what if you were making 1% off of 100 people's effort vs 100% of your own? I was dumbfounded, I resigned from my position a week later and I never looked back. I've been a business owner ever since. If someone tells you it's easy, then go talk to someone else cause being an entrepreneur is not for the faint of heart.

Step One: An Idea

I once heard Warren Buffet say do a business that attracts the masses and take the earnings from that and do something that ignites your passion. Too often, I see people that start businesses do what they've always dreamed of. That's exciting but you still have to bring in income. I started buying cars at wholesale and selling them retail. My first deal made me almost $2,500 in profit and my second deal made me about $7,000 in profit. I was essentially making what the dealership made plus the scraps they paid me for selling one of their cars (25% to 30%).

The wholesale/ retail business is great money but for me I saw another void in the same industry I was good at and that was training and recruiting. I can tell you neither is my passion but it made me great money on my own terms. I now use this money in turn to do the things that I have a passion for. Remember a majority of all millionaires have several different streams of income. They don't just settle for one source.Write your ideas down clear and please don't quit your job if you're not clear. You don't get what you want in life, you get what you picture.

Step Two: Name for your business

At this point in the game you don't need to have trademarks or copy-rights etc. but you need to think about getting it done sooner than later. Your name needs to be something that can fit into several different genres of business and people are able to easily understand it.

Step 3: Logo Creation

Your logo is your brand, so be precise with who you get to create it. If you're working on a limited budget they have several different sites that offer individual services from people of all walks of life and countries from inexpensive to mildly expensive. You definitely can find anything that you're looking for on these particular services sites.

Step 4: EIN#/ Tax ID

This step is easy but so crucial to how you get paid and how you build business credit and payment of your taxes.

A lot of people think they have to pay for this service but it's free. Go to IRS.GOV once on the site go to APPLY FOR AN EMPLOYEE ID NUMBER, then click on APPLY FOR EIN ONLINE. The site will take you through the steps. You can only apply during normal business hours. I suggest making your business an LLC (Limited Liability Company) and make sure it's an S Corporation (you'll thank me later ☺).

Step 5 : Registering Your Business With Your State

Filing your business within the state you live in is imperative if you want to get paid legally. Most banks require this before you can get a business bank account. This is usually for a small fee typically no more than one hundred dollars. You're going to need a business bank account, trust me. You never ever want to get paid via your personal name or your personal bank account. It's much easier to build business credit when you mess up versus building your personal credit when you mess up. In some instances, you can just start over completely. Remember it's called a Limited Liability Company for a reason. Remember most businesses fail within the first year, failure in business is a good thing, learn from it and don't ever get discouraged. Keep it moving and develop that Rhino skin.

Step 6 : Website / Social Media

Depending on the business that you're in, a website is imperative and it's always good to link it to all of your social media platforms. Social media is a great tool for business. I love Instagram and Facebook as well as YouTube (videos are key). We have a global marketplace now, so if you're not connected to social media with your business, you're missing out on clientele. Figure out who your target audience demographic is and hit those people first and create a sales funnel. When you first start , it may seem overwhelming and extremely scary. I often get the butterflies in my gut as well whenever I begin a new business venture. I recommend a book called: Before You Quit Your Job by Robert Kiyosaki. Starting my business was well worth the risk and the reward is far better than the pain you're going to go through. This will be a new life and a new beginning. NEVER EVER QUIT!!!

KHATIB ALI

LESSON 5
NEGATIVITY IS VIRUS

I speak about this all the time. I'm going to break it down scientifically, so you can understand where I'm coming from. Negativity is simply energy. There are two types of energy - positive and negative. So, I want us to look at ourselves as human beings. We are made from the atom. The atom is made up of energy. There is the positive portion and the negative portion, which makes us. I consider the positive portion God, and I consider the negative portion the devil. And it's a battle within ourselves.

There is fear and fearlessness. Fear is negative, fearlessness is positive. Good and bad. And the reason I call it a virus is because when you speak negativity, when you release that energy of negativity, you infect everyone and everything around you including your subconscious. You can't try to mix oil and milk. It doesn't work. So, I tell people all the time, that you have to go in every situation with a positive mental attitude. Believe me I understand that we are humans, we are going to have some negative times and days. But when you think positively, positive things will become attracted to you, because positive only attracts positive and negative only attracts negative.

Let's do this, I want you to go out to your car and open the hood - take your jumper cable and plug it up to the battery of someone else's car and hit the positive cable to the negative cable on the other car. What's going to happen? BOOM! Please don't really do this!:) So, positives and negatives do not attract. So, how do we continue to stay positive? Some people meditate to stay positive. I look at the most beautiful things in my life. Both of my daughters - I have a picture of both of my daughters and when I look at those pictures - I understand why I am going through or growing through the situation and I become positive again. And I understand who and what I am doing it for.

So, let's speak about the devil. I am not a preacher, I am not your spiritual advisor, but I understand the devil to be negative. I understand that anytime I feel like I can't achieve something that it is the devil whispering in my ear. And we all know how the devil works. So, what I encourage you to do, when that negativity creeps up, is to become a rhino. That's where thick skin comes in - that is where that cut off the arm notion comes in - to protect you against negativity. If you're around four broke people, you're number five. If you are around 4 broke negative people, you are the 5th broke and negative person. If you're around 4 broke negative ugly people, you are number five. That is the worst situation you can be in life.

There is nothing worse than being broke, negative and ugly. I'm not just talking about financially broke. I am talking about broke spiritually, broke mentally, and broke physically. I want you to understand, that negativity is the worse disease, ever created, in this universe. So, I encourage you to have a positive mental attitude. When you have a positive mental attitude, this helps you become more successful, it helps you break through the walls of negativity, it helps you surround yourself with people as successful and more successful than you.

Because as the saying goes, if you are the smartest person in the room, you are in the wrong damn room. One thing that helped me get out of the negative trap - was watching my surroundings and who I surrounded myself with. I used to always be in trouble. It seemed like trouble followed me. Because every time I started my day, I thought the world was against me, I thought the "man" was against me (whoever that was) - I thought the tax system was against me, I thought the government was against me.

I blamed every single person, for everything I went through instead of looking at myself. So, when I was looking at my surroundings, I started to change my surroundings. Cut out the TV, I cut out the friends that weren't going places that weren't really my friends. I took my sexual energy, and I put it into things more constructive. A man that thinks the same way, in his 20's as he does in his 30's has lost 10 years of his life. So, start surrounding yourself with people that want to uplift you.

Start thinking that you can conquer anything and nothing is in your way. No boundaries, no ceilings. Start dressing for the job that you want, not the job that you have. Stop settling and start believing that you can have everything that you want and that there is always light at the end of the tunnel. One of my favorite books of all time, Think and Grow Rich by Napoleon Hill. There is a story titled 3ft from Gold, and it talks of a man who just didn't believe.

He got excited he found speckles of gold and after not finding any for some time he gave up. And when he gave up, he sold all of his equipment. And the difference between him and the person he sold his gold digging equipment to is attitude. So, after buying the equipment he took over with a good positive attitude, with the same equipment and more determination, he became rich overnight. And all it took was 3ft. I tell you this story (because I want you to read Think and Grow Rich). I want you to understand that your greatest success is right around the corner, from your greatest adversity.

KHATIB ALI

LESSON 6
FAILURE VS SUCCESS CONSCIOUS

Failure Conscious Definition:The continued thought process of failure or worry on a specific task or plan...

Success Conscious Definition: This is a state of mind where you cannot and will not see yourself as anything else but a success. This does not mean you might succeed, it is a definite guarantee of success...

Many people in life don't realize they are operating from this particular state of mind in regards to failure conscious. It's basically a person that rarely experiences anything good, they don't believe in themselves, and they feel they will fail at any and every task they undertake.

It starts from birth, the things that we are taught as a youth from our parents to our grandparents, then it transitions to school from kindergarten to high school - we are taught to get passing grades. If you don't get an A+ you aren't as good as everyone else. If you get a C you're mediocre. And God forbid you get an F, because now you are a failure. So, the way we are taught all through school, is failure conscious. School is set up, into a way of learning that's designed for us to be robots. That's why most A students end up working for D students. So, what we need to understand is that our makeup all through life has made us the person that we are. But failure is good, because without failure, there wouldn't be success.

Let me give you an example. We all know who Thomas Edison is - but we all don't know his story. I will give you a brief summary. When Thomas Edison was working on inventing the lightbulb, a lot of people don't know he failed. He tried over 10,000 times to invent the lightbulb. How many of you would have continued trying to invent a light bulb that you didn't even know was a light bulb if you had failed even 5 times? Thank God it was Thomas Edison, because on his next try he managed to complete our first expression of a light bulb and had he been failure conscious - you would be reading this book right now under candlelight. So, I want you to understand what I'm sharing with you, growing up, I was told by my teachers, because I was a C student. That I wasn't going to be successful, that I wasn't going to amount to anything.

And then, when I came home with those C's and my older brother came home with all of those A's, I heard the same thing from my parents. If you keep getting grades like this you will be nothing but a garbage man. And I know there are people that grew up in similar situations as myself. So, all through life, I thought I was a failure. Until one day, my sixth grade science teacher, I will always remember him, told me that I was special and I could do anything I wanted in life regardless of what other people told me. And that stuck with me for a long time. I often tell people, that even though there may not be many people cheering for you on down here, all of heaven is rooting for you. So, how do we break failure consciousness? How do we teach our kids not to be failure conscious? You might think this is funny, but every single morning I look myself in the mirror and believe me I'm human, so sometimes it's hard, and I tell myself - you are the greatest.

And you are here for a purpose. Because God doesn't call the qualified, He qualifies the called. I do this same ritual with my daughters. And this is what you have to understand about the 3% of the population that are Rhinos. Either they are fearless and move with success consciousness or they have been raised or mentored by someone that taught them how to be success conscious. There was a great book I picked up years ago, and it was called Rich Dad Poor Dad, by Robert Kiyosaki. The premise of the book, was what his rich dad taught him and what his poor dad taught him. The poor dad who was his biological father was extremely educated, had all kinds of degrees, but still managed to be a part of the 97% group.

While his rich dad, barely had a high school diploma, owned his own business, and became one of the richest men in Hawaii. One thing that helped me break the mold from failure consciousness to success consciousness was even though I didn't have a mentor at the time, I was able to gather a Mastermind group of people I wanted to be like and I studied those people. You don't have to know them. But without mentorship and guidance, without personal development, you will keep running laps around the decks of the titanic. People always say I'm making ends meet, when they truly don't understand that ends will never meet because they are going in two different directions! Many people know I'm a big Adidas fan. And the reason I am is because of Adidas story.

Allow me to briefly share it with you. There were two people on two different sides of the planet that were scared and fearless at the same time. One was the owner of Adidas, and the other was Jesse Owens. One's business was about to collapse because he lost funding and the other was coming to a world where he was hated totally, Nazi Germany. But these two didn't let failure consciousness stop them from success. So, the owner of Adidas, Adolf "Adi" Dassler, waited at the Olympic Stadium and asked Jesse Owens, to wear his shoes, at one of the most pivotal moments in history.

Jesse Owens became the first black man in history to be offered a shoe contract from a major company and the first black man to win 5 gold medals in Olympic history at that time. But this one act of fearlessness set these two up on a collision course of success and tremendous legacies. So, what I ask you to do, is watch your thoughts, they become words, watch your words they become character, watch your character it becomes your legacy. So, all through your life, if you've gone through hardships, if you've gone through certain circumstances, where people told you, that you weren't good enough.

Then understand that you are good enough and that you can begin to change your life, and break the conditioning of being failure conscious. So, even though my 11th grade math teacher couldn't stand me, and told me I was going to be anything but successful, I managed to erase that negativity when she tried to hold my diploma and keep me from graduating, just because I didn't want to conform to her way of teaching. I remember the day that she kicked me out of her class and I told her I don't care what you think about me, I don't care how you feel about me.

I will be successful. So understand, that no one holds the power to your purpose besides you. More people by definition, some people by nature, are more positive than others. It begins with their personality. However, anyone can learn to develop success consciousness. If failure consciousness comes up in your life, you need to realistically assess the situation and be in non-resistance to it. Only allow thoughts and feelings that will help you in the direction that you want to go, you need to delete, eliminate, and destroy any thoughts and emotions that will not help you succeed. And never ever, allow your mind to dwell on negativity.

LESSON 7
JUST DO IT

You don't have to be great to start, but you have to start to be great. Keenan Ivory Wayans (Creator of In Living Color) had a discussion with his father before he really got into his success. He told his dad he wanted to be a comedian. His dad said, "son don't you want to finish college, so you have something to fall back on." And Keenan replied, Dad I don't want anything to fall back on, because if I had something to fall back on I am always going to be looking back. I prefer to look forward.

And we all know what happened after that. He is credited with one of the most successful careers in show business and one of the most successful comedy shows in television history. I tell you his story because that story hit home for me. Sometimes we just have to jump out there. We have all heard the saying, take a leap of faith. But how many of us, truly understand what faith is? The definition of faith is the complete confidence in someone or something including yourself, so I ask this question do you have faith? Faith also translates into the word fearlessness.

Do you truly have faith? And I want you to really think about that question? You can say I'm faithful, you can say I believe, but most dreams are left in the graveyard. And we pass by it every day. We see the failures and we see the successes, but yet, we still doubt ourselves. Faith simply means that you believe that you are going to be successful. So just do it! Regardless of the hurt, regardless of the obstacles, regardless of the No's, regardless of if you're "ready". If you say you have faith then trust in that faith. You see, there are a lot of people in this world right now, that have big dreams, but there is a small thought that is preventing them from going after their dreams.

It keeps people from writing down their goals. And a goal is simply a dream with a deadline. So from this point after reading this book, when these pages are closed, I want you to have faith that you can get out there and accomplish what you want to accomplish. And I'm telling you this, it's not going to be easy, it's not going to be quick, but I can guarantee you, the reward is going to be so much greater than the pain that you are going to go through. So, I want you to imagine yourself as a rhino, thick skin, when you walk the ground shakes. You've been a rhino so long, that you grow a horn. And imagine, going after your goals, is like being in the jungle.

You have so many obstacles in your way. But as a rhino, you move all those obstacles. You have everything going against you, yet with that thick skin and that horn, you manage to make it all the way through the jungle to paradise. And when paradise happens, it's like you are on a cloud watching yourself and your accomplishments. And when you have a piña colada in one hand and your loved ones in the other doing whatever they want to do, you are going to understand, that all those trials and tribulations, all those setbacks, the electricity getting turned off, eviction notices coming, cars getting repossessed all of that "shit" was worth it. Because, I will tell you that all of that is going to simply be a memory. So, just do it. Whatever your heart desires, step out there with unwavering faith and laser focus, that whatever you are setting out to accomplish, is going to manifest in your life. So remember, the time will never be just right.

I want to share something personal with you that I don't share with a lot of people. When I got out of the Marines, my life was in limbo. I wanted to go into law enforcement because that's all that was offered to me at the time. During that time I got into a little bit of trouble, more so a lot of trouble HA!, that kept me from getting into law enforcement. So, I started in this company called Dial of

America, and this company gave me my first taste of sales. They paid me $10 an hour, and for every sale that I got, because we were selling - internet based services equipment, they paid me $25. I can tell you, every time I got off of work, I sat in my car and it was like a prayer service. And every time I got to work the next day it was like a prayer service.

What I mean by prayer services is you are sitting in your car talking to yourself before or after work, dreading you have to go to work or dreading you will have to return the next day. I have a saying, if you do something and every week you say to yourself "I'm not happy", then you need to immediately change what you're doing. So one day, I took a drive, didn't care if I was late to work and I was driving by a Lexus store, and something told me to pull in. I walked inside with confidence and a positive mental attitude, and said I wanted a job. And this is when my life changed. The general manager of that Lexus store looked at me and said I like you, but you are too young to work at Lexus right now. And he walked me right next door, to the Toyota store, and to make a long story short, years later I became one of the top Toyota salesman in the country. So I say all of this to tell you- get out there and just do it!

KHATIB ALI

CONCLUSION
FINAL INSPIRATION

When I first developed from a cow to a rhino, I went through several hardships in my life. One of the hardest things I ever went through in my life, while I was achieving success at the same time, which is how I founded the name of my company, Achieving Success Together. I found myself in a neonatal intensive care unit. But before I was there with my oldest daughter, before she was born, the doctors told me that my child had a 50/50 chance to live and she might not even make it to term. I was 23 years old and I didn't know what congenital diaphragmatic hernia - which was their pre-birth diagnosis of my oldest daughter was.

This is when faith came into play. Because 8 long months, we were faced with whether or not our daughter was going to live or die. But something in my heart gave me the courage to understand that my daughter was going to live, so on that eighth month my wife at the time, was flown to Winston Salem Baptist Hospital, where I was faced with the scariest situations of my life. Which was supposed to be one of the most joyful moments of my life, and that was the birth of my daughter. So I can tell you, when I was at that sink washing my hands to go into that delivery room, all I could do was have faith. And I will tell you, I was happy.

I knew that even though no one else knew because you could see everyone's face, looking at me as if when my daughter came out, she would not be alive. But I will tell you, me understanding what I know now about being a rhino, is that if you believe, then nobody else can change God's plan for your life. When my daughter came out and screamed the biggest cry you ever wanted to hear, because the doctors told me she wasn't going to do that, I knew from that point, she was going to live. So I am going to leave you all with this, it doesn't matter what people say, it doesn't matter what your surroundings are, the only thing that matters is you. So when you look in the mirror, you have to understand, that the God in you, will create whatever heaven that you want.

If you have faith, and fearlessness. So hopefully, cows versus rhinos means to you what it meant to me on that day, when God proved the doctor wrong. So be a part of the 3% club. Be part of a movement of prosperity. Get out of the rat-race and start living the lifestyle that you've always dreamed. You deserve it. Remember it's easier to be rich because there is less competition, you are only competing with 3% of the population. The money game is easy, because all we simply have to do is channel it in our direction. When you are going after your goals and dreams, remember why you are doing it.

Be willing to, metaphorically, sell your arm and be unselfish about your goals, dreams and about your legacy. Set out to be your own boss, stop helping make other people rich, because if you don't live out your dream, you are definitely going to be living out someone else's. Take negativity out of your life, because we know it's a virus that will spread rapidly and destroy your potential to succeed. Remember to develop success consciousness, versus continuing to be failure conscious. Remember to get out there and take a leap of faith. And like Nike says, just do it! Remember instead of being herded throughout life, and being on the 40/40/40 plan, and ending up being slaughtered like a cow, be that rhino that will help you smash through everything that you want to be and everything that you will be!

CPSIA information can be obtained
at www.ICGtesting.com
Printed in the USA
LVHW030911111119
636963LV00006B/2512/P